I want my book to tell a story within itself.

I want to show my pain, my healing, my redemption, my happiness, and my peace.

This 2020 edition was published by Sovereign Noir Publications, LLC
in Arlington, Virginia, U.S.A.

Paperback ISBN: 978-1-952987-06-9

eBook ISBN: 978-1-952987-07-6

Illustrations by Trina Lafargue and Anthony K. Gervacio

Somethin' Bloomn'

A POETRY COLLECTION

Myhesha Doneve

Sovereign Noir Publications

*If it's not
always happy,
it ain't love.*

-Trina Lafargue

Part One

I'VE BEEN PLANTED

Mom's Poem

I'll never forget that 2:45am call from my mother. It was like it just happened. She was hysterical and my stepfather had another one of his episodes and had to be rushed to the emergency room. I remember her saying, "Len came in the room and said Joanne call 911! I can't breathe and he was clinching his chest." About 3:15, the phone rings again and I answer, all I hear in the background was, "I'm sorry Mrs. Cawthorne, we did everything we could, your husband is gone."

My mother screams in pain and I hear the nurses trying to console her. Meanwhile, I scream, and as I'm writing this, the tears roll down my face. This is the second person close to me that took their wings to be an angel with God.

This poem is dedicated to my mother. She lost her better half when I was dealing with my own personal losses.

She is alone like me, but the difference is she lost her true love. And me, I am still waiting for mine. I am sad for her and although she has visitors that tell her they are sorry for her loss; I sit alone wishing I had someone to hold a conversation with. She will have her peace eventually and it will get easier in time. I am afraid that I will not have mine but I shall continue to be as patient as Job. I have lost a lot, but God has blessed me with so much more. I'm learning to be thankful even when being lonely is so painful at times. She will always have me, and I will always be there when she needs me. My heart aches for her but she is strong, and she will survive. She is my mother who lost her husband...

For my mother, Joanne

Garden Heart

My soul is a secret garden and
My heart is buried there
Laid to rest from all the despair
The roots of my love are the deepest,
Full of mystical secrets
And I'm not easy and neither is my heart
I know if you're lying or
Being genuine from the start
Most of all I crave a peace
That feels like freedom
Just waiting for the time,
I can live the love I've dreamed of

Empty Cup

Sometimes I feel like I will never be loved
Like I am destined to be alone
Never to be happy the way I know I should be
I'm always giving and never the one to receive
I'm sad and this kind of loneliness stings
Will the love I want and need ever find me?
Today, I think not
So, until then, that part of me shall be empty,
Waiting patiently to be filled

Self Ultimatum

Only for your convenience
And always an option
Your heart may be true,
But your mind is a conundrum
I feel like a genie locked in a bottle
Only to appear when they want me
I'm taking my power back
'Cause all I have is me, myself and I.
And until they're ready to
Put their cards on the line,
They've been officially benched, sidelined
And I know my heart is pure
And one thing is for sure
I refuse to be back in pieces
Like broken glass on the floor

The Void

I realized it was a void that I was feeling
I dove in like an addict and
Let it take control of me
I was his muse and when I
No longer could get my fix
My eyes were wide open,
And the truth was standing there
He fed the feeling of not having
An emotional attachment of
Not feeling loved and comforted
When I needed to be
I was able to laugh and dance
In the field of flowers for hours and days at a time
Then that high,
That void I was feeling,
Came crashing down
Damn!
This was one hell of a drug
Now I'm cleaning up my own mess
Hearing the voices telling me,
"I told you so!"

...I have no response.

Upset

I want to talk to you
But look what I resorted to
I cut myself off from the view
Now I'm feeling blue
Once again I had to choose
I'm left feeling misconstrued
Opened my heart to something
That wasn't reciprocated
Now I sit here very frustrated
So I'm keeping myself in isolation
Until I get over this devastation
It's best I keep quarantined
Until I get the heartbreak vaccine
Sorry that my feelings became elevated
I was wrong to think you'd be obligated
To want me in return
Embarrassed describes me best
Cause the feelings I have,
I can no longer suppress
I've added another hole in my chest
Cause I know now you never had any interest
So as much as I want to talk to you
Keeping away is the best thing to do
Sorry for telling you how I feel
Cause I see now with you it wasn't the real deal

Questions

There are moments I feel like
I'm wasting my time saving my heart for you
Am I naïve to think you care enough
To be the keeper of my priceless gem?
Cause its been broken and bruised
Can I trust you to protect it?
Are you strong enough to lead me?
It's a big responsibility and just know I'm worth it
I hope you see that cause I'm rare and magical
And I come with a price,
Only can be given to the chosen one

See Me

See me,
All of me,
And not what you see on the outside
See me and all my flaws
And judge me not
For you know my heart is pure
And if you look closely,
You'll see the universe in my eyes
And the sun in my smile.
See me and know that I want to be
Loved in way that feels like peace
See me and all the scars for they are proof
That hurt and pain did not break me
See me and know that what did not break me,
Birthed a stronger version of me
See me and see how I am a woman who
Loves whole heartedly
See me
Because I see you

Words of Advice

I sometimes wonder what a man thinks
When he seeks a woman to love
What does he see in her that draws him near to her?
Is he really after her heart
Or is he just seeking to feed his loins?
Can he truly profess his emotions to hurt her
Or is he cold as ice and will do what he can
To break her down to nothing?
Why do men hate to speak the truth about
How they feel to a woman
But quick to spit his rage at another man?
Doesn't he realize that a woman can bring him peace?
I guess he doesn't see he is controlled by his anger.
I wonder why he breaks her down constantly
And makes her so desolate.
All she wants is to be loved and protected,
But instead, he brings her pain.
And as her petals fall to the ground,
She is gone forever.
It is then that he sees the error of his ways,
But it's too late.
For the one who truly sees her, waters her, feeds her,
Loves her, and gives her sunlight until she blooms again.
So, men I ask, please,
Show us your truth because a man without a queen is lost
Remember she can be the cure to all your pain
Or the poison that brings you to your knees
Choose wisely how you treat her,
Because all she wants is to be loved the right way.

Heart's Wish

I am the venom and the antidote
Complicated yet simple
I crave peace that I've yet to know so I'm protecting my
heart and watching my words
My thoughts are mine, so I keep them to myself
Seeking the provider, protector and leader called man.
He will be the one who will take the lead,
Show me the way and I'll submit and follow
With him I'm not afraid cause he values and
Treats me as a woman should be
In return I will be his peace of mind,
The diamond in his crown
The moon to his sun and the stars to his universe
I will finally have my peace because my peace is with him

Frequency

I see love around me everyday
I feel the vibrations and
I can see how it makes people feel
I'm just waiting for it to happen to me
I want to have a turn to experience and
Embrace it
To allow it to set my soul on fire
Because love is breath taking

Random Thoughts About Love

I think true love and soul mates existed a long time ago when people had pure hearts and true intentions.
They could hear the beating of the others heart and that is what drew them together.
Now in a time when there is only hate, love doesn't seem to exist. Those pure hearted people cant feel or hear the signals of the ones they are intended to be with.
They have to settle for the fake and therefore become empty vessels because of their unhappiness.

Fragile

It's not easy for someone to catch my vibe
I'm hard to tame
At times I can be a mystery
I keep myself private like my history
I'm censored in all kinds of ways
Be careful with me
I'm fragile and I can be easily broken
Don't have time to be picking up
Pieces of myself again off the floor
My heart is guarded, my soul jaded
I don't speak easy
Most days my mind is a battlefield
Just want to be destroyed instead of
Self-destructing
I'm fragile so be careful with me

Efflorescence

I want to be held but in a way that is
Mentally and emotionally connected
When I look into his eyes, he will see all of me
And as he leans in to kiss me,
He holds my hands above my head
Gentle is his touch,
At that moment my flower blooms
And he penetrates me with his love
I finally feel safe and
He understands my universe.

Cortney's Poem

This poem is dedicated to my son Cortney. He showed me first what a mothers' love really is and I am blessed that God gave him to me. This poem came to me after I almost lost him, one of the four most precious gifts I've ever received. They say when the paramedics showed up, you were cold as ice and taking your last breath. They gave you all the medical attention to help but you left this world 3 times. In my cries to God and prayers, you awoke as if nothing had happened. You had a long road to recovery, but you made it through.

I love you,
Mom

Before the world got a hold of you, you were mine
So pure and innocent
My angel, my best friend
You could do no harm, but the devil tried to take you
He told me his plan in a dream when I was pregnant with you
You were just a seed inside of me and he almost succeeded
I almost lost you twice
By jail and by death
You were gone a few minutes, but prayer is powerful
God said no! It's not his time to go,
I have something for him to show
He said that you are special and
That you are going to be great
But first you must walk this path that is placed in front of you
A lesson, it's part of your fate
So, I'll continue to be a praying mother
You will shine and when it's time, this I know
Cause God said so, it is already written

Phoenix

They thought the pain would break me
They thought they could break my mind and my spirit
But they broke the wrong parts
They took my wings instead,
Thinking it would stop me
They forgot I had claws!
With a vengeance, I rained down hellfire
Clawed my way out of the darkness
Fought every demon with my crown still intact
My energy was too much for them
And they gave in
I took back my wings and transformed
Into a stronger version of myself
Unstoppable, never needing batteries to recharge
Walking into my destiny with confidence!

Testimony

My body is a temple
In my sanctuary you will find my love sitting at the alter
If you come hear my message,
I can teach you a lesson
Let me baptize you in my waters
And when you are done praying,
You'll be so thankful
Ready for communion and to be blessed
My love will have you feeling brand new,
Ready to testify and confess
And I know you want to be sin free,
Believe in miracles
I'll have you being spiritual
So, come sit with my love at the alter
I promise it'll never make you falter

Art

She was broken
She used to be in pieces
She put herself back together, differently I might add
Her light still shined but it flickered
She yearned for the one who could truly see her
The one who will help her shine brighter
And when he does finally see who she really is
He will know that she is a beautiful masterpiece

Head Over Heart

He keeps his heart and head separate, I don't know why
I want to know the answer, instead I am denied
I want to understand what he needs
I want to help him fulfill his dreams
To know what he wants and feels
To understand how he loves and the parts he keeps
Hidden inside him
I want him to show me his heart,
Even though I know it has been scarred
I want to be the one who heals that part,
To be beside him
To be the one he confides in
Help him fix his crown
So, he can continue to walk proud

Escape Plan

I'm screaming inside
I'm trying to break free from
What others want me to be
Trying not to be a statistic
Pleasing people has me motion sick
And to think I do what I do from the heart
I just want to leave because of this negative life
I don't want any parts and I'm trying to fix me
People just hate to see me be me
I'm trying to rebuild a different life for myself
To leave behind all the hate and strife
I'm tired and I'd rather just be left alone
Cause everyone is self absorbed
The blame is on me though,
I allowed it all to happen
So I cant complain about these mishaps
The truth is that while I was busy helping others,
I forgot to help myself
Now I'm falling apart and I just want
What's best for me
It's time I help and love myself
Letting go of everything else is a must
It's the only way I will be alright
Leaving everything and everyone behind me
So I can figure myself out and heal
I have no one in my corner and it hurts
I have grown thick skin for a reason
I'm the one they never cared about from the beginning
I've been used and abused for the last time
All the memories and words have been lies

Somethin' Bloomn'

It's time to say goodbye
I'm done with things not being reciprocated
I need to find my roots and replant them to grow
To bloom into something different
I'm tired of all unhealthy things
I want healthy people, places,
And situations for myself
I see why I'm so guarded and why I isolate,
Nothing is real
And until I am shown otherwise,
I don't believe anything
No expectations,
No disappointments

Authenticity

Being my authentic self has not been free
It cost me years of hurt and pain
Breaking down walls, taking off masks,
Many nights of tears
Depression and
Anger and
Countless hours in therapy
In pieces... heart, body, and soul
But here I stand... free
No more shit holding me down
No more asking permission to exist
I exist on my own terms now
I've found my worth and
My jewels are priceless
If you are not here to add to me,
Then move on!
I no longer have time for people
Who subtract from me
I'm on a journey to greatness
And I would be dumb to waste this
New found inner peace
The peace that doesn't have me in pieces
But that which gives me a piece of mind
To be my authentic self... to be me.

Silo

When the dust of the day settles,
You truly know if you're alone or not.
In my case I've always been alone,
Even when people around me,
I just feel alone.
It used to hurt but once I picked up
On other people's vibes and energy,
I realized that it was best to be in solitude.
Some friends became foes
I realized their negative energy was
Affecting my life in a toxic way
I burned every bridge just to protect myself.
And the ones that remained
Are the ones that never hurt me,
They always had my back.
We've become a close knit family,
But at times I feel alone.
So the true test lies here,
How can Myhesha be alone
Again and be at peace?

Shelter

My therapy is called pen and paper
And it is there that I am safe.
No judgment,
I say what I want without
Explaining what I am feeling.
All my fears, angry rants, and happy moments
Come alive on paper.
I am the author and I decide
How the stories begin and end.
My words give me peace
And I'm always relieved once I'm done.
It's my own world that I escape to
When the stresses of life try and hold me down.
I become a mystery,
A little fact, and some fiction.
And although my cover is dusty
And my pages are worn,
I am so worth the read.
So, lose yourself in my company,
I'll take you places you've never seen.

Somethin' Bloomn'

Part Two

I'VE BEEN WATERED + GIVEN SUNLIGHT

SALVAGEABLE

INTERTWINED

SYNERGY

TO BE

HALCYON

EQUAL

COMPLETION

HESITATION OF HAPPINESS

CONFESSING TO A SUPREME BEING

METAPHORS

SAFE HAVEN

CONFLICT OF LOVE

ADDICTION

REMEDY

UNREQUITED ADDICTION

FIGHTING

SURRENDER

UNCAGED

TRAPPED

RANDOM MOMENT OF REALIZATION

WOKE

THE MOON

CRASHING

SOMETHING REAL

MAKING PEACE WITH MY BROKEN PIECES

EPIPHANY

STRENGTH

ONWARD

LIFE ON REPLAY

Salvageable

It's the only one I have
It's been broken a few times,
But it is still warm with a few tender spots
Those spots,
I'm still trying to fix
But I love regardless of being so volatile
Cause loving takes risks,
So I guard it to keep it safe
My mind talks to it to keep it
Focused and in place
The two work together to keep me intact,
Keep me thriving
It is what I need to survive
So, I am faithful to my heart,
It's the only one I have
Still warm, broken a few times
But all mine

Intertwined

You inspire me to love
To be open and free
No balls, no chains
I shine my light as if I were
A disco ball reflecting in all directions
Peace and contentment are all I feel
The frequency of your love
Carries me away and the synergy
We create is everlasting
This experience with you has me on cloud nine
The colors we emanate continue
To define and elevate who we are as one

Synergy

Protect me from this place
A world so cold and full of fear
Where doubt is like a virus,
But your touch is the cure
You give me strength with your love
With you I am never weak
Together we have an exchange of power
A true balance of the scales
What we build cannot be broken
No matter what comes our way
In this melancholy world we are
Free because our love is greater
Than any chaos created

To Be

To be loved
For it to be permanently
A love that lasts for eternity
For him to have a soft spot for me
Complete him because I am his rib
Fulfill me because he is my heart
A bond so deep, we can't be torn apart

Halcyon

I love our conversations
How we talk,
How we laugh,
Down to the random moments of silence
You make me smile in ways I could never imagine
With all the stresses of this world,
You love me unconditionally, flaws and all
You give me a physical and spiritual high
I catch myself on frequent clouds of nine
I look at you and I'm in awe
Never thought I'd find a love like this
You showed me that a broken heart
Can heal and what love really is
You love me into freedom and
Feed the flow of my energy
My heart is yours and you have the key

Equal

You are the equivalent of me
Together we are the sum of all parts.
You give me a peace that I only could dream of
Your essence liberates me from all that I fear
I am free and it feels good to
Spread my wings and exhale
As infinite as the stars are in the night sky,
That is my love for you

Completion

You're the glue that pieced my heart back together
I'm different and brand new all cause of you
Once a dim light,
I shine brighter than ever,
And your love saved me
I used to be fragile and with every touch
I was bruised
I am delicate so handle with me care
But when you touch me you heal me
And soothe my soul
Like we are meant to be,
And I wish I could paint our love
Vibrant colors and memories,
Your love helped to complete me

Hesitation of Happiness

Its something about you
I can't figure out what it is,
But it draws me close to you
I'm under your spell
I'm both scared and amazed
Your love has me dazed
I can be myself with you
No second guessing, no questioning
Things are just understood

Confessing to a Supreme Being

I must be honest with you
This thing between us is not about sexual intimacy,
It's more than that
From the way you touch me,
kiss me, hold me, and caress my body
Even the way you speak to me
Your mental stimulation of our
Intellectual conversations have me in awe of you
Your cosmic being shines a light in my universe
You make me feel just how a
Woman is supposed to be
You set my soul on fire
And I don't want to make our
Situation
Complicated at all by telling you this
But I love you

Metaphor

I am beside you and not beneath you
Close to your heart but you protect me
Your medicine and not your pain
I was formed from your rib and can give life
You are the sun and I am the moon
I am the diamond in your crown
And help you shine
And I strive to be a virtuous woman
You are a warrior as I am a goddess
Just as man is to woman
Even though one plus one is two,
When together we are one
And just as the stars are in the universe,
We radiate through this world spreading
Love in all kinds of forms.
I unlock your masculinity with your ego
Cast aside and you own my heart
You have the keys that unlocks
All the doors of my love
Thank you for giving me peace
While I help you be free in mind and spirit
Finally, complete, you and me

Safe Haven

You give me a peace that I don't have very often
One that is calming and gives me rest
You bring sunshine to the storm I have raging inside
A protection that allows me to be free
You pray with me, for me and protect me with your love
I rest easy because I know you are around
Your love makes me forget the meaning of a broken
heart and I'm no longer in pieces
I am whole

Conflict of Love

Have you ever made love and
It brought you to tears?
To connect to a soul to the
Point you feel like atoms merging to become one
That cosmic earth-shattering love
And when you climax it feels like
You have been reborn
That's how I imagine it would be,
But you see I've never experienced it
But I imagine that's how it will be
      DIFFERENCE
Now fucking on the other hand,
Has been most people's cup of tea
You dress it up all pretty,
Pretend to be into one another
But once it is done, all interest is gone too
Ask one another if you good and it's
Back to like nothing ever happened
But someone ends up being in their feelings
Cause they let you penetrate their world
Not realizing it was just a set up to get you all wet up,
Between the sheets
No love ever existed there,
Just a quick exchange of body liquids
Then you snap out of the illusion deciding to not share
your treasure with just anyone again
Cause you want to wait for the right one who will come
along and give you that earth-shattering love
The big boom called making love

Addiction

Your love is addictive
You are on my mind when I awake
And when I go to sleep
Whenever you leave,
I go through withdrawals
On the outside I appear to be fine,
But on the inside my mind is screaming
I am paralyzed by the love you give
So I feel it's time I need a therapy session
To cure this love obsession
Cold sweats and feverish chills
Being with you gives me all kinds of thrills
Its hard to come off this kind of high
When the love you give is hard to deny
But I need to wean myself off from you
If not, I fear I will become unglued
I need this therapy session and a doctor
So, they can figure out the proper dosage of you

Remedy

Lose yourself in me
Let me show you something never seen
Something you never had
A peace you've only dreamed
In the purest form of love
If I could trade my feelings for yours
I could experience how I make you feel
Things I do to make you smile
I want to be your peace and not your headache
Your worries about me would cease
You would understand my heart
Understand that you're my missing part
My antidote, the cure

Unrequited Addiction

There are times throughout the day
When you cross my mind
I ponder whether to call or text your line
I resist cause I know the dialogue would be dry
So, I deny the temptation with great hesitation
They say that it takes 21 days to break a bad habit
You are mine and I'm the addict
I count the days that I have these withdrawals
Because I'm done with the relapses and falls
I need you out my system
Especially since I never got to mention, I love you
But that doesn't matter anymore
Since my heart has been shattered
For being a fool for wanting you!

Fighting

I'm in the ring by myself
Every round I fight to win
No help just me
The crowd in my backyard screaming
They only want me to win if it benefits them
I'm tired and overwhelmed
I want to quit
The bell rings, 2 minute break
It's me as the trainer
Get up you got this!!
Bob and weave,
Remember, two to the body, one to the head
Now get out there and get on your shit!!
The bell rings
Back at over and over I'm fighting
When will this stop
Voice whispers, "Never, it's life"
Then it happens....
I'm down, I can't get up
I look up and see me staring over me
I realize I'm fighting myself
I reach down and help myself up
You got this Myhesha, I say...
Then I awake to the sound of my alarm clock
Time for work

Surrender

You have a side, one that you hide
Just know I'm easy and in me you can confide
I can tell you've been hurt
You hide it behind your eyes
You choose strength over vulnerability
Using your head instead of your heart
I've known it from the beginning,
But I come in peace
I'll trade your broken wings for mine
I want for your hidden side to be revived
To give you a peace so pure,
You won't remember the pain anymore
So, lose yourself in me please
Because I am the antidote, the one you need

Uncaged

You keep me safe
From the madness of this world
From the demons and flaws that I hide from
You help ease the anxiety that consumes me
Like a wildfire
You cover me with your wings
And shield me from the pain
I feel when I'm hurting
You are my peace
Your love is the key that
Sets me free from this cage
I crave your love like a drug addict
The love you give makes me asthmatic
You see me for who I really am
Your kisses set my soul on fire,
It's pure bliss
I lose myself in your company
Your love is freedom,
With no walls or chains
I am forever grateful
You are the nirvana that allowed me
To be me and free

Trapped

Sometimes I feel like I'm trapped in my own body
Constantly fighting to get out as if I don't belong
I'm busting out at the seams
Because the real me wants to be set free
And I stopped trying to fit in, I fight to be myself
I feel like a dark void and I am unsure of what I am
I am not like everyone else
I am the only one of my kind
It's lonely and scary
I cry sometimes but no one hears me
I don't want to do this anymore
I just want to feel whole
Granted, I am complete,
But I still feel like something is missing
Am I the one missing?
I am not sure at times
I'm haunted to be loved, cared, and protected
But I'm not myself
And I don't know how to calm this raging fire inside me
So, I cry alone, praying my solitude gives me peace

Random Moment of Realization

Once upon a time I was young,
Naïve and settled.
Unaware that not knowing that what I had
Settled for twice over hurt me to my core.
Now I stand here much older, wiser,
Healed and most of all patient,
Never to settle again for the unknown.

Woke

When you're damaged people think you're no good
What they don't realize is that your hurt
Being hurt unlocks your mind
You're woke,
No longer a slave to the world
You see things for what they really are
Your way of thinking is enhanced
You're in a class of a new breed
Real leaders of this world
Your spirit is free
Your third eye can see
Shine your own light and be
Part of that new breed we see

The Moon

I talk to the moon about you
Wishing on stars to have you in my view
I want a relationship like the sun and the moon
The sun brightens the day,
While the moon lights the night sky
And dances with the stars
You see like them; you brighten up my life
I want to be like the stars
And dance in your night sky
Be that shooting star you wish upon
The galaxy in your universe,
your beginning,
And your end
So, I talk to the moon about you,
Telling it all that I feel
Wishing on the stars to bring you in my view

Crashing

I wanted to be the star
In your universe
But I realized that you didn't
Want to plan it with me
And like an asteroid
I fell hard to earth
Destroying parts of me
That were attached to you

Something Real

Give me somethin' real like
Meaningful conversations
Face to face interactions,
Your dreams,
Fears,
And inspirations
I want to know you and all that you are
I don't want nothing fake,
No dry dialogue
Give me somethin' real like
Your passions and what you value
Let's talk about life,
Spend all kinds of hours
Encouraging words throughout the day,
Never running out of words to say
To be a priority and not an option
The kind of realness that doesn't leave us boxed in
Give me something real,
Something honest from you
Give me something real,
For us to have a breakthrough

Making Peace With My Broken Pieces

No matter the depression and anxiety that I deal with,
I try my best to be me.
With all the trials and tribulations,
I survived the storm.
And although it broke me,
I knew it had to be done in order
To make me the woman I am becoming.
There are days that I just don't want to do anything
But God gets me going.
I'm different and my light shines brighter
Than it ever has.
I'm grateful and thankful for this journey
And for the people that I can lean on
When I need help.
So as I said, I am making peace
With my broken pieces.
Each piece is a different part of me
That reminds me of what I went through,
A memory of what I did to get through.

Epiphany

Much to my surprise
I realized how much my heart cries
Only in the nighttime,
Being with you heals the pain
Cause that's the only time I can stand the rain
Never felt this with anyone before
You are the one my heart and soul yearns for
Never felt so balanced and at peace
You make all the darkness in my life cease
Especially since you know things are
Not always easy for me
Thanks for making me one of your priorities
So, the next time I realize my heart is about to cry
I'll think of you and everything will subside

Strength

Created in HIS image,
I am the descendant of the first woman
I am a goddess,
A warrior,
A mother, and
A survivor
I was built not to quit
And strong doesn't begin to describe me
Pain was meant to break me,
And a transformation is what happened
A better version I became,
Like a phoenix reborn from the ashes,
I rise and though I am but little,
I am FIERCE because I am a woman

Onward

Getting out my own way
When you been through what I been through
You will see people and places in a different light
Reading between the lines, all I see is gray
The real story is what you see
Nothing forced so no pressure to make diamonds
Just organically flowing in this melancholy world
Everyone wants to take on the same shape
Afraid of their own form
But I love me and all my imperfections
Not trying to fit in, I'd rather standout
Be that rarity, that anomaly, that's me
Getting out of the way shall I go
Swimming upstream is how to flow
All I want is positive vibes
Enjoy life and happy to be alive

Life on Replay

I'm always holding the grenade
And pulling the pin
Always self-destructing,
Hoping to return stronger and better
I've been in pieces so many times,
It's hard to believe that I still function
My tears burn because I'm a ball of fire
Quick to burn down any bridge that's not for me
Had enough of fake love and lies
I want love but I'm not sure how to manifest it
No one knows how to be real
They are too consumed by social media and texting
I need face to face conversations
And skin to skin interactions
Intellectual intimacy that leads to laughter
To be a priority and not an option
Guess if I'm going to be at peace,
I will be at peace with myself
I'm safer with myself
I can't let myself down
Cause I love me too much

Somethin' Bloomn'

Part Three

I'VE BLOOMED

SHE

BECOMING

MASKS OFF

WALLS UP

BEAUTY OF LOVE

REDEMPTION

THE FEELINGS YOU GIVE ME

FREEDOM

UNSHACKLED

I AM

MIRRORED

HIS VIEW

BLOOMING FOR YOU

CANVAS COLORS

BLISS

THE AWAKENING

VINDICATION

HAPPILY EVER AFTER

She

She is powerful.
She carries herself like she's walking with purpose,
Standing straight up, back at attention,
Wearing her crown of confidence as if
The prize that her eyes are on is already hers.
She is untouchable.
She wants to maintain peace in her kingdom,
Desires to remain in her zone,
But don't get it twisted...
She does have an army to protect her from
The jealous ones who
Try to come for her throne,
Those who want to dim her light, and break her,
And censor her role, and slander her name
Because they think that she wants their spot.
Little do they know that she is a conqueror
Breaking down walls of stigmas,
Using her staff as a symbol of her sovereignty.
Riding out on her chariots,
In her own lane focused on herself and her tribe,
Her energy is too strong for small minds
As she swims upstream.
She is not asking for permission, she's telling you.
She's coming to take her place because it's time—
Not because you say so—
But because she knows so.
And just like a phoenix from the ashes, she rises
On a journey to greatness.
It would be foolish to waste it.

Becoming

It scares me the way I love you
This feeling is something I've never felt
You give me peace and you reciprocate
This draws me closer to you
You help me elevate and I am spreading my wings to fly
Never knew love could be so pure
I'm content and feel myself glowing with happiness
If this is how it feels being in love,
I want this feeling forever cause I'm complete

Masks Off

You show me pieces of you
The ones I know you hide
The pieces of yourself,
Of your feelings inside
I want to let my guard down completely
With you
But part of me is afraid that
You will withdraw when I do
You show me pieces of you,
Please show me your side
I'll show you my pieces too,
So no longer will we need to hide
Revealing ourselves will bring healing
And not harm
We will be unmasking who we are
So, let's share our pieces,
All the ones that we hide
Let's share our pieces,
It's time we let them shine!

Walls Up

Sometimes I stare in the mirror to see
If the scars have faded away
All the years of pain,
I hid myself in shame
I was afraid to speak
Afraid of what people would think
I walked with my head held low
Fake smile on my face,
I put on a show
I am breaking down these walls
Standing up for me
Tired of being down,
All I want is to be free
I took back my life
Doing things my way
I am not afraid anymore,
Not afraid to be me!

Beauty of Love

It's a beautiful thing
When a woman is loved wholeheartedly by a man
It's nothing that she wouldn't do for him, her king
She becomes his peace and will go to war
With anyone who tries to destroy their bond.
She no longer has those walls up like she had before
He came in and prayed for her and with her
He protects and shows her that he values her
Most of all he loves her through all her imperfections
She no longer has to hide and be guarded,
She is finally free

Redemption

With every tear came redemption
My darkest and lowest moments,
God told me I'd get through it
I had some good days and bad days
I was embarrassed of myself,
Couldn't look at my own reflection
I was broken, no light nor love was in me
Fake smiles to hide my pain,
I carried so much shame
With crying and prayer, came a tiny bit of peace
Because for me to heal,
I must release all the negative energy I had inside
And with each day, things got better
I started to do things I was once afraid to do,
Like smiling and being social
I even started to let my guard down, just a little
Always observant though,
I knew how far not to go
It's time I forgave myself for
Accepting less than what I expected
I take deep breaths, medicate,
And as the tears come pouring down my face
I know who I am,
I will never let my peace,
My worth be disturbed again
And I say to myself,
"I love you; you are strong,
And you will get through this".
I have redeemed myself
It's been a journey, but I will always be patient.

The Feelings You Give Me

You make me feel so much like a woman
I love the way you hold me,
Touch me,
Kiss me,
And caress my body
Its heaven, like atoms merging
And with you time seems to stop
I crave the peace you give me,
It calms all my storms
You are my safe place,
My shelter from the rain
Thank you for seeing me

Sincerity

My intentions are sincere
I want him happy, no longer hurt, and worried
For his mind to be at peace
To be his volt and the one who stands by him
Like a queen
I want to be his encourager,
Comforter,
And most of all,
His equal
I want to be his help mate
And the one who cures his pain
Be the one who compromises
And builds with him
I want to have an unconditional bond
Deeper than the ocean
I want to be his queen,
The one who will go to war with anyone
Who tries to destroy him or our bond.

Freedom

I never thought anyone could love me
In this moment, this very second, I feel free
How I always wanted things to be
You walked in and changed my world around
And just like Brandy, I just want to be down
I've met my match and found my equal
No sequel, I'm finally able to be me

Unshackled

If I opened my heart, would you like what you see
Or would you see a problem and flee
From all the pain that I carried inside
It's all I had that helped me survive
On the bad days, I thought I would die
I pushed myself harder, I had to try
Too much was at stake
So, I stood tall and took my place
In this life you only get one shot
So, I'm giving it all, everything I got
I don't look like what I been through, thank God
I have it all thanks to Him and he took care of the job
So, if I opened my heart, would you like what you see?
It's just me, a woman, who broke free

I Am

If you look in my eyes
You can see the universe
The twinkle you see
Are stars forming
And my smile lights up a room
It is the sun that I carry
My laughter is the coolest breeze
On a hot August day
And my being carries
Peace and positive vibes
I am the calm after a storm,
The cure to your pain
And if you shattered me into pieces,
My heart would still beat
I am contagious and pure
I am love

Mirrored

His peace…
As he looks into her eyes
He is enlightened
In awe of her beauty in spiritual form
He finally has someone he can adore
REFLECTION
Her peace
She looks into his eyes
She feels so empowered
In awe of a cosmic being
Now she is part of his universe

His View

I want to see my beauty
Through your eyes
To experience myself
From a different point of view
To see the energy that I emit to you
I want to understand my own soul
I know I'm flawed,
Yet you accept me in my true form
And I just wanted to see why...

Thanks for the view

Blooming from You

As you look me in my eyes,
Help calm my spirit
You quiet those busy
Thoughts that plague my mind
Understanding my soul
As you read my pages,
You decode me like a hidden message
I like to lose myself in your company
And while you give me peace,
Accepting all my imperfections
You are my freedom which has
No walls or chains
You see me for me
And every morning I birth
A new version of myself
Like a lotus flower
All because of you...

Canvas Colors

This happiness I feel
I wish I could paint it
To show you how I've healed
Colors so vibrant and bold
It's the love and memories
That are shown
Your essence liberates me
From all my fears
You give me a peace
I use to dream about
And just when I thought
I wasn't capable to reciprocate
You shined your love
And I bloomed like a flower
I'm completely open,
Liberated,
And free

Bliss

Never felt a love like this
So innocent and pure
You are the one I adore
Couldn't ask for anything more
Your kisses, hugs, and touch
I've never felt so safe
Everyday is eternity with you,
It feels so right
To fall asleep in your arms
And awaken to your kisses
I'm blessed that God sent you
Finally have the love I've dreamed of

The Awakening

Every time I looked into their eyes,
It wasn't love I would see but uncertainty
You would have thought
I saw all the red flags
But I was blind,
Believing false words
And fake illusions
Should have known that
I wasn't safe
But my feelings wouldn't
Let me escape
I looked in the mirror
And didn't recognize
My own face
Allowed the wrong people
To sample me
Without paying the fee
Once I finally awoke from my trance
I was bare,
Broken and in pieces
But I put myself back together,
Differently i might add
You see I found my worth and
Dropped all that was bad
Never catch me looking back and
Turning into a pillar of salt
On a new level now

Vindication

I swore i'd never follow in
My parent's footsteps
Yet, i woke up years later
And saw i did just that
A history of drugs,
Alcoholism,
And physical abuse is where i came from
The perfect combination for failure
But i vowed for redemption
I wanted my soul to be cleansed
To experience real love,
To be truly seen and not lied to
I wanted the kind of love where
I didn't need to wear my seat belt,
Cause the driver knows
He has precious cargo
So, i did the hardest thing in my life,
I forgave myself
I asked god to forgive me,
He washed away my sins
Clear is my path now,
I can finally be me
I chose to love me first,
Before i love someone else

Happily Ever After

You can't keep popping up in and out my life
Causing me to put my heart on pause
I'm not some non-disclosure or a clause
If you can't decide what you want, please leave me out
I'm walking away this time with no doubts
I have my own priorities and goals to master
I'm my version of happily ever after

Somethin' Bloomn'

Myhesha Doneve

Somethin' Bloomn'